is for Psychology

is for Psychology

by
Natasha Schvey

Illustrations by
Nicole Jones Sturk

For Gavi, my tiny muse.

And for my Dad,
who taught me how to read.

xo

First Printing, 2019
ISBN 978-0-578-46818-1

The images were created using vector design and the text was set in PT Serif Caption.

A
is for
Attachment

B is for Brain

C is for Classical Conditioning

D is for Delusion of Grandeur

E is for Extraversion

Totem and Taboo

Civilization and Its Discontents

The Interpretation of Dreams

Jokes and Their Relation to the Unconscious

F is for Freud

G is for Groupthink

H is for Happiness
L
is for Law
by Veronica Goodman

I
is for
Inkblot

J is for William James

K is for Melanie Klein

L
is for
Learning

M is for Mindfulness

N is for Nature vs. Nurture

O is for Object
Permanence

P
is for Psychology
B = f(P, E)
APA Publication Manual
The Principles of Psychology
Diagnostic and Statistical Manual

Q is for IQ

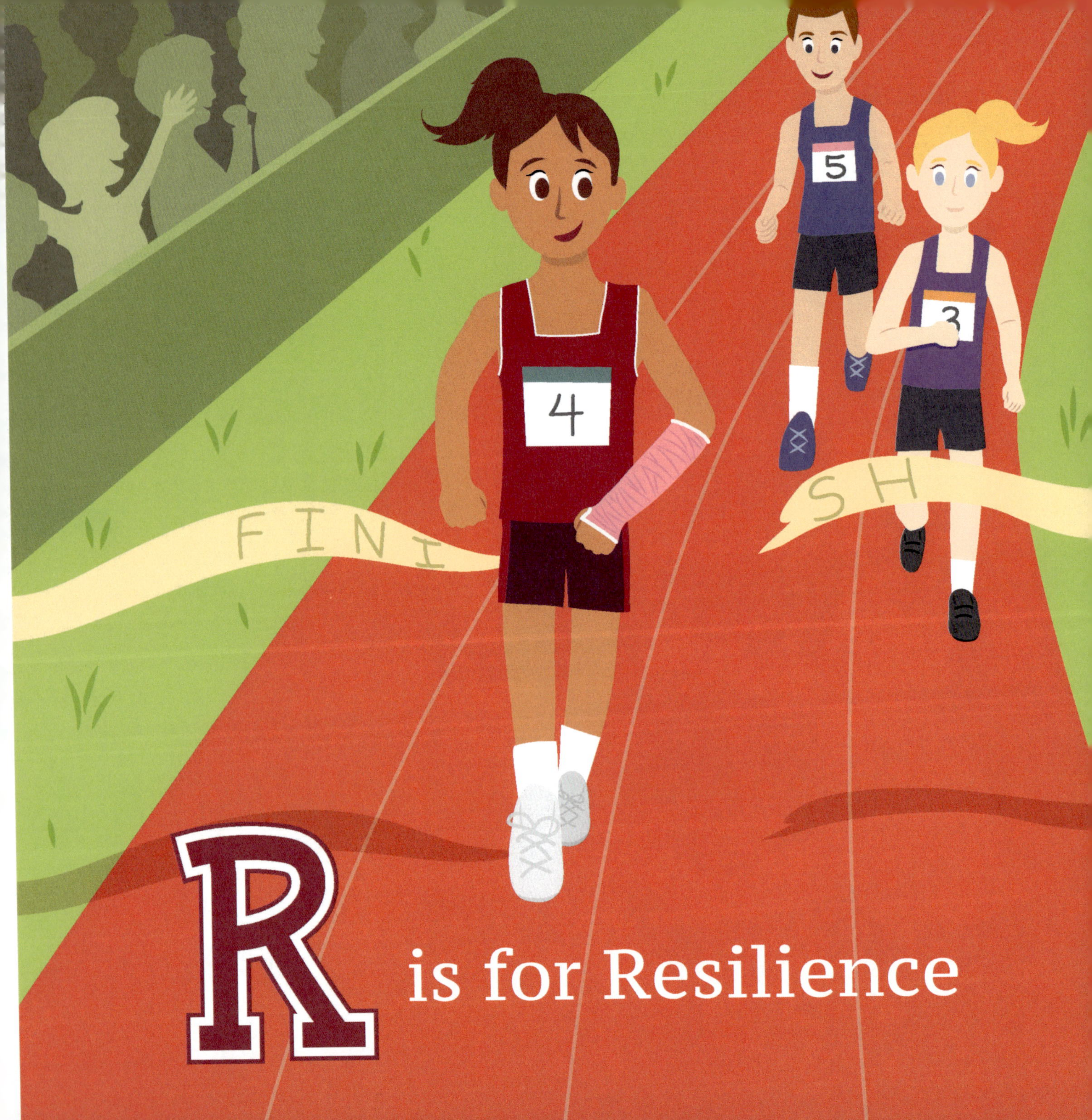
4
5
3
FINI
SH
R is for Resilience

S

is for
Self-awareness

T
is for
Therapy

U
is for
Unconscious
DIRECTOR

V is for
Visual Illusion

W is for Working Memory

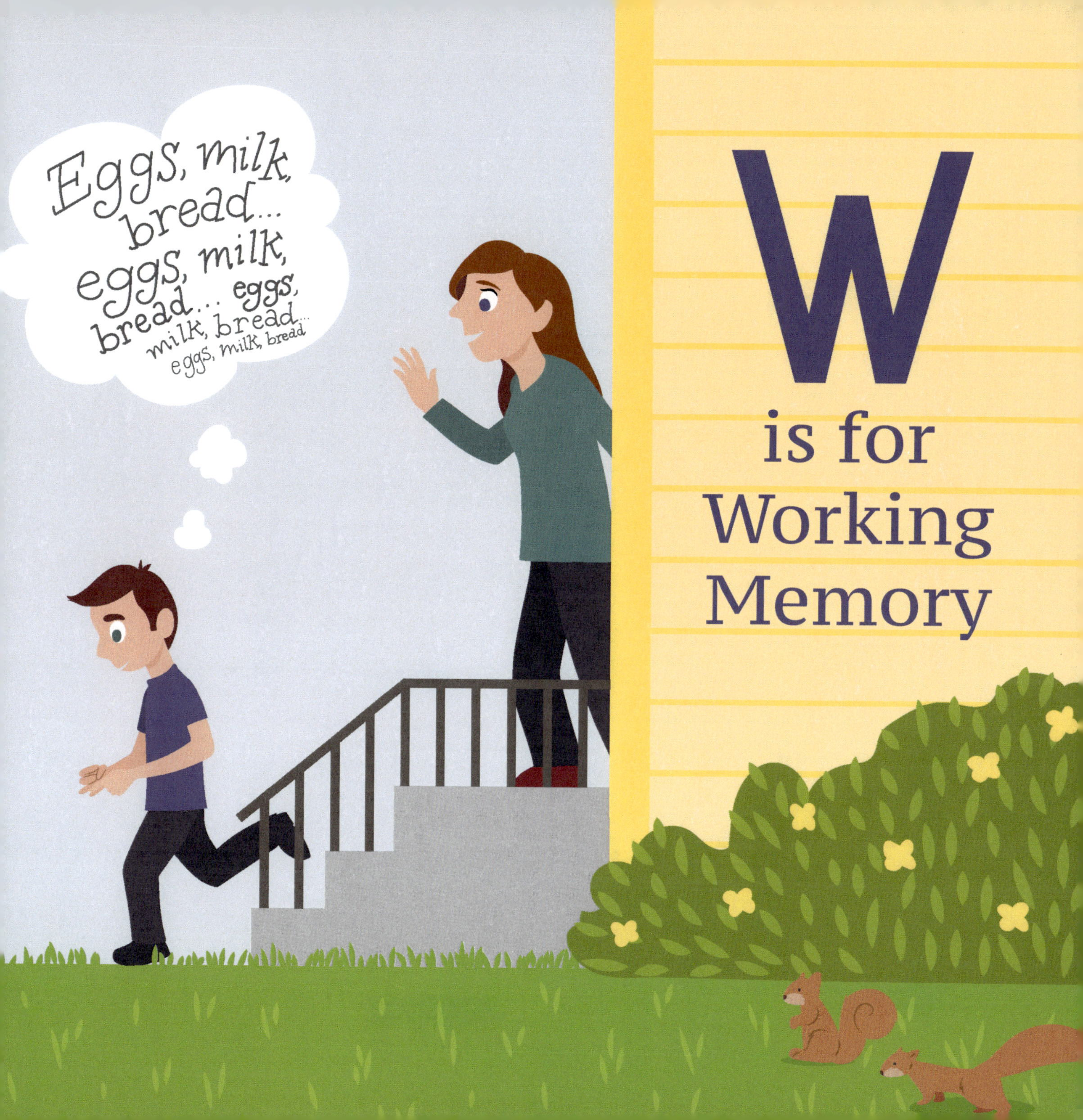

Eggs, milk, bread... eggs, milk, bread... eggs, milk, bread... eggs, milk, bread

X is for eXperiment
Marshmallows

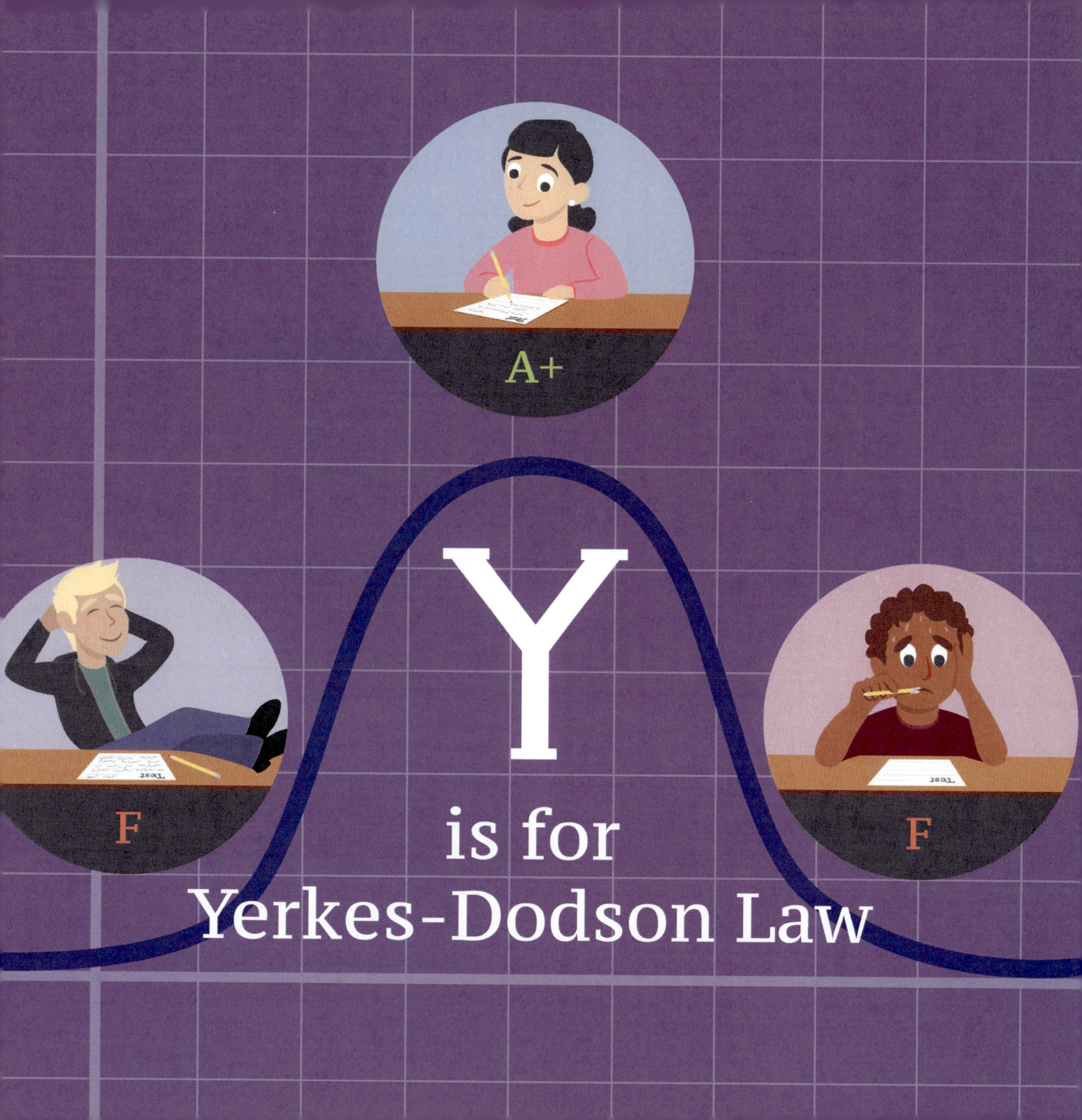
A+
F
F
Test
Test
Test
Y
is for
Yerkes-Dodson Law

Z is for Zone of Proximal Development

Glossary of Terms

Attachment The strong emotional bond between babies and their parents or caregivers.

Brain The complex organ that serves as the control center for the rest of the body. It is responsible for movement, all of our senses, and thought, as well as lots of other things.

Classical Conditioning A type of learning that occurs when something neutral (the sound of a bell) gets paired with something that makes a person react (the sight of bacon may make someone drool). After a while, the neutral thing by itself elicits the response (drooling from the sound of the bell alone).

Delusion of Grandeur When someone thinks or acts like they are much more powerful than they really are.

Extraversion A personality trait. Extraverts are usually outgoing, talkative, and may enjoy being the center of attention.

Sigmund Freud (1856 –1939) An Austrian doctor who developed a lot of famous theories about child development, why people do the things they do, and why people have certain emotions. He also developed psychoanalysis.

Groupthink The tendency of people in a group to conform in order to avoid conflict. This sometimes leads to poor decision-making or choices that are not in someone's best interest.

Happiness A state of well-being, contentment, or joy.

Inkblot Also known as a "Rorschach Test," an ambiguous inkblot pattern is shown to someone and they are asked to describe what they see. Their interpretation of it is thought to provide information about their personality and emotional state.

William James (1842–1910) Considered the "Father of American Psychology," he wrote The Principles of Psychology and taught the first psychology class in the U.S. He also developed a theory of emotion and used the example of a person running away from a bear to illustrate it.

Melanie Klein (1882-1960) An Austrian-British writer and psychoanalyst, she developed new treatments to help children, including the use of dolls and toys in therapy.

Learning The process of gaining new skills or knowledge through experience, observation, or instruction.

Mindfulness A state in which one is focused nonjudgmentally on the present moment and one's thoughts, feelings, physical sensations, and environment in that moment.

Nature vs. Nurture A discussion about the influence and importance of biological/genetic factors (nature) and environment (nurture) in shaping development. Psychologists now agree that *both* are important and cannot be separated from one another.

Object Permanence The ability of a child to recognize that an object (or person) continues to exist even if it is out of sight or hidden. This developmental milestone occurs within a baby's first two years.

Psychology The scientific study of the human mind and why we feel and act the way we do.

IQ IQ stands for Intelligence Quotient, a measure of an individual's cognitive abilities.

Resilience The ability to persevere (or not give up) in the face of difficulty.

Self-Awareness The ability to recognize oneself as distinct from one's environment and other people. This usually occurs around 18 months. Self-awareness allows us to examine our own thoughts, feelings, and behaviors.

Therapy The process in which a mental health professional works with someone to help them feel better and grow stronger, overcome a difficulty, or learn new ways of problem-solving.

Unconscious The part of our mind that we are not fully aware of but that may affect our thoughts, feelings, and behaviors.

Visual Illusion An image that makes us perceive something differently from how it really is.

Working Memory The part of our memory that helps us remember small amounts of information for a short period of time. Repeating the information over and over again can help us remember it better.

eXperiment A scientific procedure that is conducted in order to make a discovery or test a hypothesis.

Yerkes-Dodson Law The theory that too *little* arousal (like stress or anxiety) and too *much* arousal make us perform poorly. A medium amount is best!

Zone of Proximal Development The difference between what a child can do without help and what he or she can do with the guidance and encouragement of a parent or teacher.

Made in the USA
Middletown, DE
18 May 2019